the power
of calm

Also in the series:

THE POWER OF CONFIDENCE

Sarah Jane Arnold

the power *of* calm

Find your inner peace

Michael O'Mara Books Limited

First published in Great Britain in 2025 by
Michael O'Mara Books Limited
9 Lion Yard
Tremadoc Road
London SW4 7NQ

EU representative:
Authorised Rep Compliance Ltd
Ground Floor, 71 Baggot Street Lower
Dublin D02 P593, Ireland

Copyright © Michael O'Mara Books Limited 2025

All rights reserved. You may not copy, store, distribute, transmit, reproduce or otherwise make available this publication (or any part of it) in any form, or by any means (electronic, digital, optical, mechanical, photocopying, recording, machine readable, text/data mining or otherwise), without the prior written permission of the publisher. Any person who does any unauthorized act in relation to this publication may be liable to criminal prosecution and civil claims for damages.

A CIP catalogue record for this book is available from the British Library.

This product is made of material from well-managed, FSC®-certified forests and other controlled sources. The manufacturing processes conform to the environmental regulations of the country of origin.

For further information see
www.mombooks.com/about/sustainability-climate-focus
Report any safety issues to product.safety@mombooks.com and see
www.mombooks.com/contact/product-safety

UK editions:
ISBN: 978-1-78929-852-9 in hardback print format
ISBN: 978-1-78929-859-8 in ebook format

US edition:
ISBN: 978-1-78929-889-5 in hardback print format

1 2 3 4 5 6 7 8 9 10

Cover and design by Ana Bjezancevic, using illustrations from Shutterstock
Typeset by Barbara Ward
Printed and bound in China
www.mombooks.com

This book is dedicated to my clients, past and present. You amaze me with your strength, teach me through your experiences, and inspire me to learn so that I may offer you more.

Thank you for allowing me to be part of your journey, and thank you for helping me in mine.

contents

Introduction	9
In times of stress	25
Adopting a mindful way of being	33
Responding to your body	43
Responding to your emotions	55
Responding to your thoughts	73
Responding to your behaviour	91
Helpful resources	125

'the real voyage of discovery consists not in seeking new landscapes, but in having new eyes'

MARCEL PROUST

introduction

UNDERSTANDING CALM

Calmness includes the presence of peaceful feelings and the absence of challenging emotions (or any reaction to them). It's a pleasant state, evoked by our internal and external experiences, shaped by our thoughts, emotions, body and behaviours.

When we feel calm, we're not lost in anxious thoughts about the future or stuck dwelling on the past. Feeling calm is being fully alive to the present moment, with a non-judgemental, compassionate attitude. It gives the mind and body a much-needed break from the pressures of daily life.

the power of calm

When we are calm, our body is in a 'parasympathetic state', which means we're more able to rest, digest food, soothe ourselves and relax after stress. It positively influences our thoughts and increases pleasant emotions.

Frequent feelings of calm and physical relaxation in this state are associated with psychological wellbeing and improved physical health, so it's easy to see why experiencing calm is so desirable.

introduction

UNDERSTANDING STRESS

Stress, much like a sense of calm, is a universal experience. It refers to a state of psychological and physical tension brought about by challenging or adverse situations. Our experience of stress is influenced by our thoughts, emotions, physical responses and actions.

Common sources of stress include emotional, social, financial and physical pressures, as well as our own attitudes, expectations and beliefs about ourselves, others and the wider world. When the demands placed upon us exceed our ability or perceived ability to cope, we experience stress.

the power of calm

A variety of elements can support or hinder our capacity to manage stress, including our:

- physical health, diet, and lifestyle choices
- ability to regulate emotions
- time management, planning, and prioritisation
- personal history and past experiences
- relationships and social support networks
- openness to learning, reflection, and self-awareness

introduction

- beliefs about ourselves, others, and the world
- focus on the past, present, or future
- personal values and goals
- perception of stress itself
- confidence in our ability to cope and succeed

the power of calm

Stress is commonly linked to feelings such as anxiety, frustration, anger, overwhelm, helplessness and sadness – all of which can be challenging to endure.

Physical symptoms may include headaches, muscle tension, a racing heart and rapid breathing. When we are stressed, it often becomes difficult to think clearly or make sound decisions, leading to reactive and impulsive behaviours.

stress is our inbuilt threat-detection system against harm

the power of calm

When a threat is perceived – whether physical, like being chased, or psychological, such as fear of rejection – our sympathetic nervous system is activated. This system is designed for survival, preparing us to fight, flee or freeze in order to protect ourselves. While this response is typically effective for immediate physical dangers, it also signals us to potential psychological threats.

Stress is not only triggered by external circumstances; our internal automatic thoughts and core beliefs can activate the same fight, flight or freeze response. Patterns such as self-criticism or the suppression of thoughts and feelings are signs of a fight response.

introduction

Avoiding stressful situations or numbing oneself – using substances or excessive sleep—are common flight reactions. A freeze response can manifest as numbness, overwhelm, tension and an inability to take action or rest, often occurring when neither fighting nor fleeing resolves the threat.

Chronic stress harms our health by causing both physical and psychological issues. In Western society, 'disorders' are often diagnosed quickly, and doctors prescribe psychiatric drugs to relieve 'symptoms' linked to stress and past pain. For this reason, it's easy to see why stress is generally seen as something negative.

RESPONDING TO STRESS

It's unrealistic to feel at peace all the time. Some emotions, like contentment, serenity, trust and gratitude, feel pleasant and cultivate an innate sense of calm. Others, like anxiety, anger and helplessness disrupt it.

This poses a very real dilemma. If experiencing stress is a normal part of being human, how can we experience a greater sense of calm in our lives?

introduction

YOU CAN ENABLE CALM

Stress, anxiety, depression and loss can leave us feeling powerless. The more we struggle, trying to control things we cannot control, the more disempowered we feel. This guide suggests concentrating on what you can influence, while accepting what you cannot change. It will support you to:

- notice and understand your stress reactions
- cultivate a mindful way to respond to stress
- respond to your body in a way that helps you
- understand your emotions in a helpful way

the power of calm

The techniques within this book are grounded in Acceptance and Commitment Therapy (ACT), Mindfulness, Dialectical Behaviour Therapy (DBT) and Cognitive Behavioural Therapy (CBT), all of which are proven to facilitate psychological wellbeing. There are further resources on page 125.

It takes time, practice, reflection and willingness, but you can strengthen your ability to cope with stress. You can learn to enable better mental health and a greater sense of peace and autonomy in daily life.

With warm wishes,
Sarah J. Arnold

in times *of* stress

'be curious,
not judgemental'

WALT WHITMAN

in times *of* stress

NOTICING YOUR STRESS

Do you know when you're stressed? How does it manifest for you? Challenging thoughts, frustration, social withdrawal, poor sleep, lack of exercise, unhealthy diet and drinking more alcohol than usual are common indicators.

Noticing you are feeling stressed is the first step towards self-awareness and positive change. Take time to reflect on your personal indicators. Noting your feelings and realizations deepens self-awareness and facilitates positive change.

EXPRESSING YOUR STRESS

Freedom of expression is key to our wellbeing – particularly when stressed. If you're feeling blocked, or uncertain about how to express yourself, these prompts might help:

- Describe the situation. What has happened/is happening?
- How does your body feel? Are you feeling any physical sensations?
- Note your emotions. How are you feeling?

in times of stress

- Note your thoughts. What's your mind saying about this situation, others and you?

- Be aware of any automatic behavioural urges. What do you feel like doing right now?

Emotional expression can facilitate cathartic release. Making music, art and talking therapy are some examples of expressive activities that you might find helpful. It's about finding what's right for you. Different expressive activities will help different people in different ways at different times.

SPOTTING THE STRUGGLE

It's common to fight, flight or freeze when confronted with demanding, threatening or painful situations. This reaction aligns with our biological programming. Although resistance to unwelcome internal experiences can intensify discomfort, these responses are a function of the brain's protective mechanisms.

When you encounter such struggles, aim to recognize them as they occur, or as soon after as possible. You may observe a tendency to wish circumstances were different while experiencing emotional distress. It is important to acknowledge that stress and discomfort often present significant challenges.

recognize your struggle with compassion

adopting
a mindful way of
being

'be kind to yourself...
you will come to see
that all evolves us'

RUMI

adopting *a mindful way* of being

INTRODUCING MINDFULNESS

Mindfulness means tuning in to the present moment with compassion, acceptance and openness. When adopting a mindful way of being in response to our struggle with stress, our thoughts, emotions and urges are allowed to be, simply as they are. Mindfulness can be practised formally (through meditation) and informally (through an activity practised in a mindful way).

PRACTISING MINDFUL AWARENESS

With mindful awareness, you're not trying to change anything. You're simply opening yourself up to what's already there, with a compassionate, curious and non-judgemental attitude (as best you can).

Find a quiet space and practise mindfully noticing your experience. Use these prompts to guide you.

adopting a mindful way of being

- Observe your environment. What can you see, hear, touch, taste and smell? What colours, shapes and textures do you notice?

- How does your body feel? Do you notice any sensations or pains?

- What emotions are you feeling? Use one word for each (anxiety, gratitude, hopefulness).

- What's your mind thinking about? Notice your thoughts as they enter your mind, stay, change, leave and perhaps return.

TAKING BREATHING SPACE

When experiencing stress, pause and take 5 minutes. Acknowledge any resistance to your present reality. Sit quietly in an upright, comfortable position and try the following practice:

1. Close your eyes if this feels comfortable, and anchor yourself in the present moment. You might notice the surface you're sitting on or your hands on your lap. Take one full, conscious breath in – and out.

2. Tune in and acknowledge your internal experiences now, as best you can. What thoughts, emotions, sensations and urges

adopting a mindful way of being

are there? Describe what you notice (for example: 'A feeling of anxiety, worries, the urge to distract myself and a fluttery feeling in my chest'). Gently observe these experiences.

3. Place a hand on your chest and offer yourself compassion; it's difficult to sit with our stress.

4. Shift your focus to your breathing now. With each breath, you are creating space for your experiences. You don't need to like their presence; simply acknowledge that they exist in this moment. Breathe with them.

the power of calm

5. Note whenever your mind wanders with a short sentence (for example, 'Thinking about work') and then bring your mind back to your body and breath. Congratulate yourself for reconnecting with the present moment.

6. Expand your attention from the breath, to include the whole body – noticing what you can touch, feel, smell and hear.

7. When you feel ready to finish this short meditation, simply open your eyes and allow your body to stretch if helpful.

This responsive practice grounds you in the present and reassures your mind and body that, though stressed, you are safe.

you *can* choose how to respond to your stress reaction

responding
to your body

'do you have the patience to wait until your mud settles and the water is clear?'

LAO TZU

responding *to your* body

When our stress reaction is triggered, a number of changes occur. Distress signals activate areas of the brain, allowing us to perceive the threat and think fast about how we can reach safety. Stress hormones are released and our blood pressure temporarily increases, helping to fuel our bodies. Our breathing quickens, increasing oxygen to the muscles, and our muscles tense and contract – ready for action if needed. These reactions are designed to enable us to protect ourselves from possible danger.

the power of calm

In times of stress, anxiety and panic, we may take in too much oxygen. This can cause symptoms such as hyperventilation, pressure on the chest, sweating, dizziness and faintness. When this happens, we need to support the body and brain to calm down physically first.

responding to your body

When you're feeling stress physically,
begin by reminding yourself that your
stress reaction:

is normal

is not trying to hurt you

will pass

BREATHING FOR CALM

Breathing out for longer than you breathe in restores the body's equilibrium. This helps you to feel calmer.

Sit quietly and comfortably in an upright position, or stand, and:

1. Breathe in through your nose for the count of four. (Counting on your fingers if helpful.)

2. Hold the breath for a second.

3. Breathe out through your mouth for the count of six. (A long, firm breath out.)

4. Do this for several rounds. Yawn to finish and deepen the practice.

your body and
breath are anchors
in the ocean of
your mind

RE-BREATHING FOR PANIC

Feelings of panic may lead to hyperventiliaton, when you try to take in too much air or gasp for breath. Use the effective technique opposite to rebalance your oxygen and CO_2 levels – calming your body and brain:

responding to your body

Cup your hands over your nose and mouth to create a seal.

●

Breathe slowly – in through your nose and out through your mouth.

●

Breathe your exhaled air like this until you feel your body settle or you want to stop.

●

Remind yourself that feeling panic is a normal reaction to an abnormally stressful situation. It will pass.

EXTERNALIZING PHYSICAL PAIN WITH VISUALIZATION

Step 1: Settle and sense

- Find a quiet space and gently close your eyes.
- Bring your attention to your breath, allowing it to anchor you.
- Notice where the pain resides in your body. Let yourself be curious about it.

Step 2: Visualize the pain

- Imagine the pain as a separate entity in front of you and ask:
- What shape does it take? (Jagged? Blobby? Geometric?)
- What size is it? (Tiny like a pebble or vast like a boulder?)
- What colour and texture does it have? (Fiery, black and smooth? Pale and wispy?)

responding to your body

- If you're experiencing multiple types of pain (e.g. burning vs aching), repeat this for each one.

Step 3: Dialogue with the pain

- Ask the pain: 'What do you want me to know?'
- Notice if it shifts shape, colour or intensity as you engage with it.
- See if you can add something supportive to your image of the pain. (For instance, you might imagine a heart to signify compassion for yourself; an open window for fresh air; a blanket for softness and support).

Step 4: Re-integrate and reflect

- Open your eyes slowly.
- Note down what this was like for you as a practice, and feel free to use it again if helpful.
- Did anything shift emotionally or physically?

responding *to your* emotions

'when a painful or even a pleasant feeling arises, the truth is – it is there. Any resistance only causes more suffering to arise'

THE VENERABLE
BHANTE VIMALARAMSI

responding *to your* emotions

Human emotions are a normal, universal experience. We feel them all for different reasons. Our emotions are influenced by our circumstances, other people, our perception, memories, beliefs and fears. Knowing why we have emotions can help us to accept and understand their existence. Our emotions, as raw and unpleasant as they can be, serve an important function: they are messengers, designed to tell us important information about our thoughts, needs and experiences. They can motivate us, prepare us to take action, warn us about possible threats to our wellbeing, enable us to protect ourselves, communicate crucial things to others and prompt others to respond to us.

Different emotions communicate different things – which is why it's so important to name what we're feeling. Here are some examples of human emotions and what they may communicate.

Fear warns us that our mental/physical wellbeing could be threatened. Without fear, we would not survive as a species. We may need to take action to manage the perceived threat and do things that give us a sense of control, comfort and safety.

Sadness often conveys that we've lost something of importance. Unexpressed anger can manifest as sadness and turn into depression. In response, we need to be gentle with ourselves, acknowledge our pain and do things that give us a sense of pleasure and mastery.

responding to your emotions

Anger communicates that we've been treated unfairly, or we believe a situation is wrong. Underneath anger there is often sadness. We may need to be mindful, assertive or problem-solve in response to it – rather than lashing out at ourselves and others.

Happiness is an emotion that comes and goes. It typically conveys that our reality matches or is exceeding our expectations; we're being accepted by others, and we're experiencing a sense of pleasure/competence with particular activities. We may want to keep doing the things that evoke this feeling and think about how else we can experience it.

the power of calm

From an early age, many of us are given invalidating messages about our emotions and their expression; you might be familiar with responses such as:

'Don't worry about it'

'Stay strong'

'Don't cry'

'Be brave'

'Don't be scared'

'Stop feeling sorry for yourself'

These messages give the impression that we should be happy all the time, we shouldn't feel or express our more challenging emotions – and we should be able to control them.

responding to your emotions

As a result, many of us believe there is something wrong with us if we're feeling sad and anxious; we may begin to view our natural human emotions as a sign of personal weakness.

Challenging emotions can certainly *feel* negative – they're designed to get our attention and can feel unpleasant and overwhelming.

Fortunately, managing our emotions is a skill. With self-compassion, patience and practice, this can be mastered. Changing how we think about and relate to our emotions is key.

The next few pages detail some fundamental concepts to reflect upon and practise.

CHANGING YOUR LANGUAGE

Support your mind to understand that your emotions aren't inherently bad or dangerous by calling them 'challenging emotions' rather than 'negative emotions'. Challenges require effort, patience and perseverance, but they can be managed effectively.

Practise this when you think or speak about your own emotions and the emotions of others. Your body may still exhibit a stress reaction, but adopting this perspective can soothe stress.

the language we use to describe our experiences shapes our experiences

UNDERSTANDING HOW FEELINGS AND THOUGHTS LINK

Our thoughts evoke feelings, and feelings trigger thoughts. These thoughts reflect our emotions, our perception of a situation (but not always the facts), our fears and beliefs. Feelings can be described using 'feeling words' (one word for each emotion). For instance:

sad	frightened	angry
anxious	happy	calm
annoyed	hopeful	panicked
overwhelmed	distrustful	shocked

responding to your emotions

Whenever you're experiencing challenging emotions, practise noticing the link between your feelings and your thoughts. For example:

I am feeling: overwhelmed, helpless and anxious.

My mind is telling me: 'I can't do this; I simply can't cope.'

Distinguishing between our feelings and thoughts helps us to understand their impact and respond to them more easily.

THE 'NAV' TECHNIQUE FOR NAVIGATING CHALLENGING EMOTIONS

It's normal to want stress to go away, but struggling with emotions doesn't help. Naming, accepting and validating emotions has many benefits:

1. Naming our emotions causes the brain to release neurotransmitters which soothe and calm our stress reaction.

2. The brain feels heard. The emotion doesn't need to get louder and stronger in order to convey its message.

responding to your emotions

3. It creates space for you to decide, with a clearer mind, when and how you want to respond to your emotions.

4. When we're feeling calmer, we can think more clearly and address the issues that triggered our emotions in the first place.

5. Self-compassion, acceptance and self-validation are associated with good mental health.

the power of calm

Here's a step-by-step guide to help you navigate your emotions, as and when they arise:

First, pause. Notice you're feeling emotionally triggered.

Take a mindful breath – in through your nose and out through your mouth.

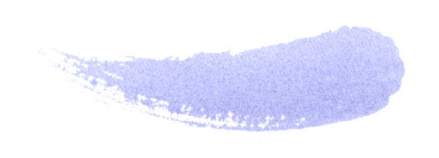

responding to your emotions

With each emotion you're feeling, see if you can:

Name it.

Use one word for each emotion. For example, I am feeling:

- angry
- anxious
- frustrated
- sad

Accept that this exists for you right now.

Acceptance does not mean liking. You can't control how you're feeling, and you don't need to. Breathe with your feelings and the sensations they bring, making room for them with each breath. Acknowledge them and allow them to be with you. Remember, they're not trying to hurt you – and they will pass.

the power of calm

Validate your feelings.

Practise observing your emotions without judgement. You may understand what's triggered them – or you may not. Validate your experience by reminding yourself that you're human, and you're allowed to feel your feelings.

Notice if you're feeling feelings about your feelings. For example, we can feel scared of our sadness; NAV these too!

Remind yourself that what you're feeling is real and important.

responding to your emotions

NAMING YOUR EMOTIONS

If you're not used to naming your emotions, this may feel difficult at first. Try using something called a 'Feelings Wheel' – an accessible diagram that can help you to identify your emotions with greater ease. See page 125 for one you can download and use.

responding
to your thoughts

'the greatest weapon against stress is our ability to choose one thought over another'

WILLIAM JAMES

responding *to your* thoughts

Thoughts are psychological events that manifest as words, images, ideas and memories in the mind. Moment by moment, we experience **automatic thoughts** as reactions to internal and external triggers. In addition, we all possess attitudes and beliefs that build up over time. These may or may not be conscious, but they affect how we think, feel and act.

the power of calm

Thinking enables us to comprehend the world, develop a sense of self, maintain relationships, problem-solve, create and thrive. It's no wonder we listen to our thoughts, believe them and react to them (a process called **fusion**).

Fortunately, we have the capacity to consider our thinking (a process called **metacognitive awareness**). We can learn to observe our difficult thoughts, 'unhook' ourselves from their content and change our relationship with them (a process called **defusion**). This helps us feel a greater sense of calm and control during turbulent times.

responding to your thoughts

NOTICING YOUR MIND THINKING THOUGHTS

As it's an automatic process, we only really notice our thoughts when they're evocative. Practise noticing yourself thinking on a daily basis – when you're not particularly stressed. For instance:

- Notice your mind thinking specific thoughts. For example, 'I'd like a cup of tea.'
- Notice your mind doing something, like planning. For example, 'What am I going to buy for dinner tonight?'
- Notice what your mind is thinking about – topics such as work, friends or family.

Being aware of your mind thinking thoughts enhances your metacognitive awareness.

NOTICING AND NAMING STRESS-RELATED THINKING STYLES

Our thinking changes when we're emotionally triggered. Over time, automatic thinking styles become habitual and can be detrimental when unnoticed. Here's a list of common ones:

Black-and-white thinking: Seeing one extreme or another, and not recognizing the nuances in between. For example, believing something or someone is all good or all bad.

Catastrophizing: Believing a situation is far worse than it actually is. It's common to imagine the worst outcome will happen.

Comparisons: Negatively comparing ourselves to others. For example, thinking we're not as good or as capable or as attractive as they are.

responding to your thoughts

Emotional reasoning: Viewing a situation based on how we're feeling. For example, 'I feel scared; something bad is going to happen.'

Empty positive thinking: Reassuring ourselves with phrases like 'It'll be fine' can invalidate our emotions and interfere with our ability to manage situations, because it encourages us to ignore what's bothering us.

Filtering: Focusing on the difficult/unwanted aspects of a given situation – forgetting to consider the pleasant parts and the bigger picture.

Jumping to conclusions: Making assumptions, judgements and predictions about a situation and reaching unwarranted conclusions. We might assume that we know what someone else is thinking or why they behave in a particular way.

when a belief hinders you, see it for what it is – a build-up of past pain or fear

responding to your thoughts

Mood-dependent retrieval: Having thoughts that match with our current mood. For example, we're more likely to recall depressive memories when we're feeling sad, and more likely to recall pleasant thoughts when we're content.

Over-generalizing: Making inaccurate, generalized statements about how things are. For example, 'This always happens.' In reality, it may happen a lot, or it may not, but it doesn't *always* happen – there are exceptions.

Worrying: Feeling anxious about real or hypothetical situations, often fearing uncertainty. We tend to exaggerate threats and doubt our coping skills, which can trap us in an unproductive cycle without solutions.

the power of calm

Ruminating: Thinking in a repetitive way about something that has already happened. There may have been an undesirable outcome or something didn't go as we'd hoped. This thinking style often links with self-criticism, unfair self-blame and 'shoulds'.

Self-critical voice/internalized bully: Putting ourselves down, criticizing and bullying ourselves. For example, we might label ourselves 'stupid', 'worthless' or 'useless'.

Shoulds: Regularly thinking or saying, 'I should,' 'They should've,' 'You should' etc. can put unreasonable pressure on ourselves and others, creating unrealistic, unachievable expectations.

Personalizing: Relating things back to ourselves, often blaming ourselves for the things that could go wrong – even though we're not responsible (or only partly responsible) for the outcome.

responding to your thoughts

Make a note of which stress-related thinking styles resonate with you.

Most of us will experience some or all of them from time to time. They're a natural consequence of:

- the way our minds work
- stress and fear
- past pain and past experiences

the power of calm

We can disentangle ourselves from our difficult thoughts – and reduce their impact – by noticing and summarizing them as and when they arise. Here's how:

1. Tune in to your thinking as soon as you notice challenging emotions or bodily sensations.

2. Notice what your mind is telling you. What thoughts are popping up?

3. With a mindful attitude, you might say: 'There's over-generalizing!' or 'Ah, that's a self-critical thought.' Use the stress-related thinking styles to help you.

With this awareness, you can choose to continue with what you were doing, or address the issue/s arising in a more grounded way.

with awareness,
your thoughts
are less likely to
influence you in
an unhelpful way

THOUGHT DEFUSION

Here are some more defusion techniques to try.

Mindful appreciation of your brain

Anxious thoughts are the mind's way of protecting you from harm. When you next experience them, appreciate their function; your brain is keeping you safe. Decide for yourself how you want to behave.

Identifying past pain and/or fear

We believe particular things about ourselves, others and the world. Sometimes these beliefs help us ('I'm lovable'); other times they hinder us ('I'm useless'). When a belief based on past pain or fear hinders you, see it for what it is: 'That's past pain talking' or 'That's fear talking.'

responding to your thoughts

'I notice I'm having the thought that ...'

See if you can put the following phrase in front of your thoughts whenever you get emotionally triggered: 'I notice I'm having thoughts that ...' For example: 'I notice I'm having the thought that she doesn't like me any more. That's painful.'

This simple technique helps you remember that you are thinking thoughts and they may not be 100 per cent true or helpful. If they are true, you can think about what might help you or the situation, but only when you're ready to.

NOTICE YOUR LANGUAGE

The language we use influences how we think, feel and act. Consider the difference between the stress-related automatic thought, 'I can't cope,' compared to: 'I'm feeling overwhelmed and finding it hard to cope.' The former suggests the individual can't help themselves and may prompt them to behave in ways that unwittingly reinforce this belief.

Consider the alternative thought. Notice how this language reflects the individual's reality, but in a way that opens up space for autonomy. When you're feeling triggered, adjust your language as required.

responding to your thoughts

QUESTION: IS IT HELPFUL?

When we get emotionally triggered, our thoughts can become reactive and unconstructive. The next time you notice this happening, ask yourself one or more of the following questions:

- Does it help me to fuse with this thought?
- How would I act if I believed these thoughts? How might I act if I didn't?
- What would a self-compassionate response sound like? What do I need to hear right now?
- What would I say to a close friend if they were facing this situation or having these thoughts?

responding *to your* behaviour

'be resolutely and faithfully what you are; be humbly what you aspire to be'

HENRY DAVID THOREAU

responding *to your* behaviour

In times of stress, you *can* regain control. You might find it helpful to ask yourself these questions:

- What can I do to help myself or this situation?
- How can I best take care of myself right now?
- What do I need?

Your answers will depend on your wants, needs and the situation. In this section, we'll explore some behavioural self-help tools that enable calm and support your wellbeing.

LEARNING TO COMFORT YOURSELF

Comforting yourself can stabilize your mind and body. Also called 'self-soothing', it involves being gentle, compassionate and peace-making with yourself. This may help you tolerate pain and distress, without making things worse. Rather than reacting impulsively, it helps you respond to your emotions thoughtfully. The intention is not to get rid of them; you're recognizing they exist and responding with kindness.

You may or may not know what brings you a sense of comfort during times of stress. It can be helpful to think about activities that will nourish you in some way and appeal to your senses. For example, what comforting things might you like to see, hear, touch, taste and smell?

responding to your behaviour

Here are examples of some activities to try when you next feel the need for some comfort and care:

- Watching your favourite TV show or film in a warm and cosy environment.
- Using an aromatherapy burner for relaxation.
- Listening to comforting music.
- Taking a warm bath or shower, with scents you enjoy and soft lighting.
- Wearing comfortable, comforting clothing.
- Placing a hand on your chest and wishing yourself well.

the power of calm

Resist any urges to soothe yourself in a counter-productive way (binge-eating; excessive drinking; unaffordable spending). Escapist ways of managing stress can be addictive because they work in the short term (temporarily reducing challenging feelings). In the long term, they can create more problems and leave you feeling worse.

Allowing yourself to feel good may feel unfamiliar and a little scary. Appreciate your mind's hesitation, and do it anyway. You deserve to spend your time in ways that add value and nurture you!

allow yourself
to feel good

'WHAT'S ON YOUR MIND?': THE 'BRAIN DUMP'

This technique helps you recognize – and respond to – what may be on your mind when you're feeling overwhelmed, tangled and stressed.

1. Take an A4 piece of paper and write in the centre: 'What's on my mind?'

2. In no particular order, write down everything that comes to mind (like a mind map).

3. Now, take a moment and look at what's on your piece of paper.

responding to your behaviour

4. Writing it down creates distance and helps you compassionately understand why you're feeling overwhelmed. From here, you can respond in a logical way.

5. Reflect on what's essential to do and what's simply desirable. Highlight one very important thing that is achievable now. After completing this, you might find it helpful to tackle the next thing.

6. Don't forget to schedule in pleasurable activities, because they're essential for your wellbeing, too.

PRACTICAL PROBLEM-SOLVING

Practical problem-solving is a helpful way to deal with worries that we can do something about. This helps us experience a greater sense of calm because we're supporting the mind to know that it can cope. Here's how:

1. Identify the problem using clear and specific language.

2. Adopt an open, non-judgemental attitude and brainstorm all the possible things you can do in response to the problem. Write down each option, then consider the pros and cons.

responding to your behaviour

3. Choose your approach to the problem, and identify the steps you'll need to take in order to make this happen.

4. Check that each step in your plan is realistic and achievable, and begin when you're ready.

5. Offer yourself some genuine personal praise for addressing this. Now you have a plan to deal with the situation.

BEFRIENDING YOUR ANXIETY

Take a similar approach with anxiety. Anxiety is maintained when we overestimate the threat and underestimate our ability to cope. You can combat this by following an anxiety-management strategy:

1. Ask yourself, 'What specifically am I anxious about?' Try to be as realistic as possible.

2. Say it does happen, 'What could I do to help myself and the situation? What qualities do I have that I might lean on? What people or organizations might I ask for support?' Give yourself time to reflect, then write down your ideas.

3. Notice what happens to your anxiety when you befriend it, gently, and decide how you can help yourself and the situation. Make a worst-case scenario coping plan.

you can cultivate
the skill of anxiety
management with
time and practice

ASSERTIVENESS TRAINING

We're born with the capacity to be assertive. A newborn baby cries to get its needs met. As we get older, we find it harder to express what we think, feel and need. We might fear the consequences of expressing ourselves or have learned to communicate in passive or aggressive ways. Remembering our human rights, and practising behaving in line with them, can help you find your assertive voice:

- I am allowed to feel my feelings.
- I am allowed to express my opinions and beliefs respectfully if I want to.
- My thoughts and feelings matter, even if others don't agree with them.
- I am allowed to change my mind.

responding to your behaviour

- I am allowed to make mistakes, and I can learn to own them when they happen.
- I can choose to say 'yes' and 'no' for myself.
- I can set my own boundaries, according to what feels comfortable for me.
- I can choose to behave in a manner that respects the rights of others and myself.
- I am allowed to walk away from situations and people that harm my wellbeing.

the power of calm

Being assertive can improve our relationships with others and ourselves. It improves the chance of our needs being met. So what might assertiveness look like in practice?

- Pause. Take a breath, then verbalize what you feel in a way that's respectful of yourself and the person you're talking to.

- Speak clearly and concisely.

- Keep your voice at a constructive volume (not too loud; not too soft).

- Offer the other person your eye contact if you can.

- Acknowledge the other person's viewpoint and empathize, as appropriate.

responding to your behaviour

- Use 'I' statements: 'I think ...' – 'I would like to ...' – 'I agree ...' – 'I disagree ...'
- Highlight your experience without blaming the other person. For example, 'When you shout at me, I feel really anxious.' This is better than saying someone made you feel a certain way, as this can evoke defensiveness.
- Speak your process. For example, explain that you're not sure what to say. This will help the other person understand your internal world and reduce the likelihood of misunderstandings.
- Check in with the other person. 'What do you think about ...?' – demonstrate that you want to listen and co-operate.

the power of calm

- Disarm criticism by owning it, rather than becoming defensive. For example, 'Yes, I can be messy – you're right.'

- Respectfully disagree when necessary. For example, 'I disagree, but you're entitled to your opinion.'

- Notice your emotions and express them verbally, rather than acting them out. For example, say, 'I feel really angry with you,' rather than shouting at the person or slamming doors.

- If you're unable to contain your emotions, explain that you need some time to calm down. If you hope to be able to talk again later, say so.

responding to your behaviour

Many people feel scared that being assertive will damage their relationships. In actuality, people often find that when they speak openly and honestly with others, in a kind and respectful way, they tend to (a) experience improvements in their bonds, and (b) get their needs met more often than when they are passive, aggressive or passive-aggressive.

Learning to be more assertive can significantly improve your quality of life, decrease depression and reduce problematic anxiety. But be patient with yourself. When you've communicated in a non-assertive way for a sustained period of time, it takes a while to re-learn how to be assertive; keep practising.

PHYSICAL SELF-CARE

Diet: There's a strong relationship between a healthy, balanced diet and good mental health. Remind yourself to drink enough water, as dehydration makes stress management that much harder. Reduce your consumption of alcohol and avoid recreational drugs. They will deprive you of the chance to realize you can cope with your stress/distress without them.

responding to your behaviour

Exercise: Find a form of exercise you can enjoy on a regular basis, rather than forcing yourself to do something you don't like. Exercise significantly reduces stress levels and helps you feel more calm, confident and competent.

Sleep: Good-quality sleep (around eight hours per night) supports the mind and body to feel calmer. If poor sleep is a problem, consider purchasing self-help books (see page 127 for recommended resources). If it remains a problem, consider seeing a psychologist who specializes in helping with sleep problems.

MINDFULNESS MEDITATION PRACTICE

Formal mindfulness meditation is an invaluable activity to practise, especially when we're feeling stressed.

Regular mindfulness meditation can enhance metacognitive awareness, self-insight, gratitude, stress and emotion management, relationship satisfaction, social connection, self-compassion, compassion towards others and immune-system functioning. It can also decrease depression, anxiety, stress, self-criticism, emotional reactivity and obsessive-compulsive symptoms, and prevent depression relapses.

practise guided meditation to develop the skill of mindfulness

VALUE-BASED LIVING

Your values are ongoing principles and ways of being that reflect who you are and want to be, rather than goals to be completed. Knowing what our values are – and living life in accordance with them – can enhance our wellbeing.

At a time that suits you, reflect upon your values. They may be things that you currently embody and practise, or they may be things that deeply matter to you but are not currently reflected in your way of being.

responding to your behaviour

They are still your values, and you can align yourself with them with time, a mindful attitude and practice.

You might find it helpful to ask yourself some or all of the following questions.

- What really matters to me as a person?
- How do I want to treat myself, others and the world around me?
- What personal qualities do I want to cultivate?

the power of calm

Here's a list of some values that may help you to clarify yours:

- Acceptance
- Adaptability
- Adventure
- Assertiveness
- Authenticity
- Autonomy
- Bravery
- Charity
- Commitment
- Community

responding to your behaviour

- Compassion
- Connection
- Contribution
- Control
- Cooperation
- Creativity
- Curiosity
- Determination
- Discipline
- Empathy
- Encouragement

the power of calm

◆ Equality ◆

◆ Fairness ◆

◆ Fitness ◆

◆ Forgiveness ◆

◆ Freedom ◆

◆ Friendship ◆

◆ Fun ◆

◆ Gratitude ◆

◆ Generosity ◆

◆ Hard work ◆

◆ Honesty ◆

◆ Humility ◆

responding to your behaviour

- Humour
- Intimacy
- Justice
- Kindness
- Knowledge
- Love
- Loyalty
- Meaningful work
- Mindfulness
- Open-mindedness
- Order
- Patience

the power of calm

◆ Personal growth ◆

◆ Pleasure ◆

◆ Reciprocity ◆

◆ Reliability ◆

◆ Respect ◆

◆ Responsibility ◆

◆ Rest and relaxation ◆

◆ Security ◆

◆ Self-care ◆

◆ Self-compassion ◆

◆ Self-respect ◆

◆ Sensuality ◆

responding to your behaviour

◆ Stability ◆

◆ Supportiveness ◆

◆ Trust ◆

◆ Willpower ◆

◆ Wisdom ◆

Make a note of the values that are most important to you right now. Reflect upon what you can do to help yourself live in line with them. For example:

Self-awareness (value): I will commit to practising a guided mindfulness meditation every evening for one week (action).

Self-care (value): I will practise NAV-ing my emotions and self-soothing for the next week – and reflect upon this in my notebook (action).

IN SUMMARY

Ultimately, you *can* craft a life for yourself that you want to live. The smallest value-based changes can make a big difference. Over time, they add up and create a significant positive change. Step by step, you can explore and practise the techniques and ways of being outlined in this guide – and discover what best benefits you.

This will help you to develop confidence in your ability to cope with life's challenges – and enjoy a greater sense of calm.

You can craft a life for yourself that you want to live

helpful resources

helpful resources

Acceptance and commitment therapy
www.thehappinesstrap.com

Harris, R. and Aisbett, B., *The Illustrated Happiness Trap: How to Stop Struggling and Start Living*. Robinson, 2014

Assertiveness support
www.cci.health.wa.gov.au

Enhancing metacognitive awareness
Siegel, D. *Mindsight: Transform Your Brain with the New Science of Kindness*. Oneworld Publications, 2011

Guided mindfulness meditations
www.franticworld.com/free-meditations-from-mindfulness

Naming your emotions – the feelings wheel
www.drkenmcgill.com/2022/01/05/ten-steps-to-improve-your-emotional-self-awareness-using-the-emotions-and-feelings-wheel

How to deal with a difficult dilemma
www.actmindfully.com.au/upimages/10_Steps_For_Any_Dilemma.pdf

Introductory texts about mindfulness
Alidina, S. *Mindfulness for Dummies*. John Wiley & Sons Inc., 2010

Arnold, Dr S.J. *The Mindfulness Companion*. Michael O'Mara Books, 2016

the power of calm

Kabat-Zinn, J. *Wherever You Go, There You Are: Mindfulness Meditation for Everyday Life*. Hyperion Books, 1994

Penman, D. and Williams, M. *Mindfulness: A Practical Guide to Finding Peace in a Frantic World*. Little Brown Book Group, 2011

Williams, M. et al. *The Mindful Way through Depression: Freeing Yourself from Chronic Unhappiness*. The Guilford Press, 2007

Living well with physical pain
Kabat-Zinn, J. *Full Catastrophe Living: How to Cope with Stress, Pain and Illness using Mindfulness Meditation*. Revised edition. Piatkus, 2013

Support for neurodivergent brains
Neff, M.A, *Self-Care for Autistic People: 100+ Ways to Recharge, De-stress, and Unmask!*, Adams Media, 2024

www.additudemag.com

Mindfulness resources from world-renowned professionals
www.themindfulnesssummit.com

Responding to addictive urges
www.portlandpsychotherapyclinic.com/2011/11/riding-wave-using-mindfulness-help-cope-urges

Responding to sleep problems
Arnold, Dr S.J. *The Can't Sleep Colouring Journal*. Michael O'Mara Books, 2016

helpful resources

Arnold, Dr S.J. *The Sleep Coach*. Michael O'Mara Books, 2018

Meadows, Dr G. *The Sleep Book: How to Sleep Well Every Night*. Orion, 2014

www.howsleepworks.com/hygiene.html

'Safe Room' visualization technique for creating calm
www.donnabutler.bandcamp.com/releases

Visualisation-based meditations for relaxation
Lantham R, *Guided Meditations*. Audio CD. Meditainment Ltd, 2007

ABOUT THE AUTHOR

Sarah Jane Arnold is a Chartered Counselling Psychologist and author. She works for the NHS and in private practice, offering psychological therapy that is tailored to the individual. She supports her clients to understand their pain, break free from vicious limiting cycles and respond adaptively to difficult thoughts and challenging feelings so they can live a full and meaningful life.

Sarah lives in West Sussex (UK) with her partner Mine, their dog Maya and Priscilla the bearded dragon.

You can find Sarah at:
www.themindfulpsychologist.co.uk
www.instagram.com/themindfulpsychologist